Mel Bay's
Blues Bass Play-Along Trax

Play-Along Tracks for Developing your Blues Bass Performance Skills

By Frank De Rose & David Barrett

School of the Blues Lesson Series

Online Audio

D1733790

ONLINE AUDIO

1	Travelin' Man Blues (E)	18	Travelin' Man Blues Playing Example
2	Muddy's Shuffle (G)	19	Muddy's Shuffle Playing Example
3	In The Box (G)	20	In The Box Playing Example
4	Mr. Green (Fm)	21	Mr. Green Playing Example
5	Minor Problem (Cm)	22	Minor Problem Playing Example
6	Major Problem (G)	23	Major Problem Playing Example
7	Charlie's Swing (B♭)	24	Charlie's Swing Playing Example
8	Uptown Jump (F)	25	Uptown Jump Playing Example
9	The Stroll (F)	26	The Stroll Playing Example
10	The Key (G)	27	The Key Playing Example
11	Good Mojo (E)	28	Good Mojo Playing Example
12	Mr. Rhumba (A)	29	Mr. Rhumba Playing Example
13	Boogie (A)	30	Boogie Playing Example
14	The Tramp (C)	31	The Tramp Playing Example
15	Little Bit (D)	32	Little Bit Playing Example
16	Welcome		
17	Tuning		

To Access the Online Audio Go To:
www.melbay.com/21064MEB

1 2 3 4 5 6 7 8 9 0

Visit us on the Web at www.melbay.com — E-mail us at email@melbay.com

Table of Contents

About This Book & Notation

Welcome to the *School of the Blues Lesson Series!* This book and recording were created to help give you context to all the music you worked so hard to learn. The recorded Play-Along Trax have no bass. This gives you the opportunity to work on your blues bass patterns. I have used several different keys and tempos throughout these Play-Along Trax. These Play-Along Trax give you a very realistic example of how you would play live with a band.

Music examples are kept fairly simple to make sure this book is accessible to bass players just above the beginning level. For best understanding of these techniques refer to Mel Bay's *Blues Bass, Level 1* (MB21063BCD).

Lastly, all the references in this book are written for a right-handed four string electric bass. If you play a 5 string bass you just need to extend the examples to include your B string. If you play left-handed then you need to reverse any references to the left and right hands. We will use standard music notation along with bass tablature (TAB) for this book.

About the Author

Frank De Rose, a fixture in the California Bay Area blues scene, brings 25 years of blues bass playing experience to School of the Blues. During those 25 years Frank has been a band member with many of the area's top blues bandleaders and performers. That list includes: Gary Smith, Tommy Castro, Mark Hummel, Kenny Blue Ray, John Garcia, Mike Shermer, Sid Morris and many others. Through those associations Frank was commonly in the position to be asked to provide his bass playing skills to a long list of national touring blues performers. That list includes: Snooky Prior, Otis Rush, Johnny Heartsman, Nick Gravenites, Andy Just, Chris Cain, Rusty Zinn, Jr. Watson, Jackie Payne, Larry Davis, Mississippi Johnny Waters, Johnny Adams, Luther Tucker, Curtis Salgado and many others.

Frank's instruction approach focuses on a solid understanding of the bass player's role in the blues and a deep study of the music's tradition. He takes this core of understanding and builds upon it to teach his students the role the modern-day blues bass player is asked to play. His students actively participate in local jam sessions and bands. Through Frank's comprehensive and caring approach, it's obvious when listening to his students that he is teaching the next generation the art of the blues bass.

About the School of the Blues Lesson Series

School of the Blues is a school dedicated to the study of blues and all the styles it influenced. Founded in 2002 by educator David Barrett, the school thrives today as the center of blues education in the San Jose/San Francisco, California Bay Area.

The instructors at the school and this lesson series have on average twenty years teaching and performing experience. All of the instructors were hand picked to teach at the school for their playing skills, knowledge of their instrument and ability to teach all skill levels of private and group instruction. We are all dedicated to our craft and receive huge pleasure playing an active role in our students' musical and personal development as well rounded musicians.

This series is a continuation of this love for the blues and its education. David Barrett is the administrator and co-author of all the books. Many meetings took place with all of the instructors to shape the outline of this lesson series and to make sure that the experience and knowledge of the instructors are contained within each book.

This series is also designed for students of other instruments to play together. If you have friends that play guitar, harmonica, keyboard, or drums, tell them about this series so that you can grow together. There's nothing more fun than making music with other people.

We all wish you the best of luck in your studies. For more information about this series or to contact us, please visit www.schooloftheblues.com.

Music & Instrument Primer

Tuning Your Bass

There are several methods to use when tuning your bass. The easiest method is to get an electronic tuner designed for the bass. Read and follow the directions that come with the tuner. In short you will plug your bass into the input on the tuner. You will strike or pick the open G-string. The tuner will show you if your G-string is sharp or flat. Turn the tuning key until the tuner shows that you are on pitch. Repeat the same process for the other strings.

Along with a tuner you should have a metronome. This little device will help you to develop your sense of time. Since you do not have a drummer to play along with when you practice your scales and exercises, you will need a metronome.

The metronome establishes the number of beats per minute to be played. You can start an exercise at a slower tempo (around 80 beats per minute for example) and work your way up to a faster tempo (such as 100 beats or 120 beats per minute) as your skills develop. The metronome will be your benchmark for playing in time and a helpful tool to work on songs that need slowing down to learn.

Standard Musical Notation

Music is written on a staff. The staff is made up of five lines and four spaces. Below is an example of the music staff with the **Bass Clef**.

Ex. 1

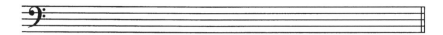

The names of the notes are the same as the first seven letters of the alphabet. The notes are written in alphabetical order. A, B, C, D, E, F, G. The lines on the staff for the bass clef are the notes G, B, D, F and A. The spaces on the staff for the bass clef are the notes A, C, E and G. Below is an example of the music staff for the bass clef with notes in place for the lines and spaces.

Ex. 2

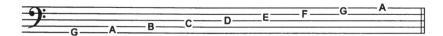

Notes can be added above and below the staff by using ledger lines. Here is the approximate range of a standard four string bass going from the lowest note, the open E on the 4th string, ending on the highest note, the D at the 17th fret on the G-string (the 1st string).

Ex. 3

An octave is the eight-note distance between any note and the next higher note with the same name. Bracketed above is the low E note to the next higher E note; this is called an octave interval. This term applies to all eight-note intervals.

The staff is divided into **Measures** by **Bar Lines**. A measure is the time between two bar lines. The **Time Signature** denotes how many beats are in each measure (top number) and which note value is to receive the beat (bottom number). Blues almost exclusively uses the **4/4 Time Signature**. For this time signature there are four beats to the measure with the quarter note receiving the beat (we'll speak of quarter notes soon). A heavy double bar line marks the **Ending** of the music. A dotted heavy double bar line is a **Repeat Sign**. You are to replay the music between repeat signs. Measures are also known as Bars as in "12 Bar Blues." At the beginning of a piece of music a **Key Signature** will be present. The key signature tells the player which notes are to be raised or lowered. A **Sharp** (#) notated in the key signature or in front of a note head (called an **Accidental** when in front of a note) raises that note by one fret (1/2 step). A **Flat** (♭) notated in the key signature or in front of a note head lowers that note by one fret. A **Natural** (♮) notated in front of a note head cancels a sharp or flat previously found in that measure or shown in the key signature.

Ex. 4

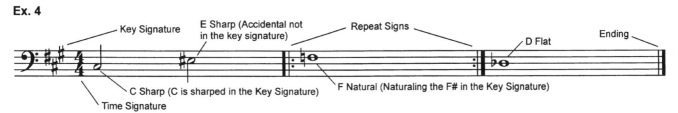

Tablature and Fret Board Diagram

Tablature, also known as **TAB**, shows the location of the notes on the neck of the bass. The four lines of the tab relates to the four strings of the bass. Starting with the lowest line of the tab equaling the low E-string (4th string) and ending with the highest line of the tab equaling the high G-string (1st string).

Ex. 5

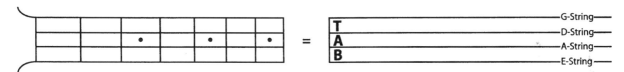

In the tab format, the notes to be played are indicated by placing the fret numbers on the tab line that represents the appropriate string. In the example below the tab is instructing us to first play the open E-string with the 0. Then we are to play the note at the 3rd fret of the E-string followed by the note at the 2nd fret of the A-string. And lastly we play the note at the 3rd fret of the E-string.

Ex. 6

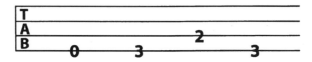

Tab is usually used in conjunction with standard music notation. The rhythms, rests, and notes are written on the top staff in standard notation. The locations of the notes to be played on the bass are shown by the tab on the bottom line.

Ex. 7

5

Rhythm Notation

Standard Note Values

The time value of a note is determined by three elements: The note head, stem and flag (or beam when multiple notes with flags are present in succession). The **Whole Note** has a head that is open and does not have a stem. The whole note receives four counts. The **Half Note** has a head that is open and has a stem. The half note receives 2 counts. The **Quarter Note** has a head that is solid and has a stem. The quarter note receives 1 count. The **Eighth Note** has a head that is solid and has a stem with a single flag (or beam). The eighth note receives a half of a count. The **Sixteenth Note** has a head that is solid and has a stem with two flags (or two beams). The sixteenth note receives a quarter of a count.

Ex. 8

Each type of note has a corresponding rest. A rest indicates that silence is to be played for a specified number of counts or beats.

Ex. 9

Dotted Note Values

If a note is followed by a "." (dot) this means that the note is increased by one half of its value. A dotted half note gets three counts. A dotted quarter note gets one and one half counts. A dotted eighth note gets 3/4 of a count.

Ex. 10

Triplets and the Shuffle Feel

The triplet rhythm places three notes where there would normally only be two. In one beat of time you would normally place two eighth notes. Triplet eighth notes fits three eighth notes in the time where there would normally be two.

Ex. 11

The shuffle feel or shuffle beat is derived from the eighth note triplet. Instead of playing three notes on the triplet we only play two because the first two notes are tied together. A **Tie** combines the duration of two notes together. In this case, you hold the first and second note of each beat together, sounding the third note of each beat separately. Blues is primarily played with a shuffle feel (called the swinging of the rhythm). For this book, this will be assumed and not mentioned from this point on. If a section is not swung, it will be noted (commonly called a **Rock Beat**).

Ex. 12

Key Signatures

At the beginning of each line of music and next to the bass clef is the area where the sharp or flat symbols are inserted to identify the key that the song is to be played in. As stated earlier, the musical alphabet is the letters A B C D E F G. For instance, a song that is played in the key of C major, the notes for the C major scale will be C D E F G A B and the octave C. When a song is played in the key of G major the note will be G A B C D E F# and the octave G. At the beginning of each line of music a sharp (#) symbol will appear on the F line. This means that the F will always be sharp unless you alter it within a measure with another symbol like the natural symbol. Then the F# is altered only for that measure or for that specific instance. The same holds true for the flat keys.

Every major key, like C major, has a relative minor key (a minor key that shares the same key signature of that major key). In the example of the C major key the notes are C D E F G A B and the octave C. The relative Minor key for C is A minor (built upon the sixth note of the major scale). The notes for the A minor scale are, A B C D E F G and octave A. As you can see the notes are the same but they are played by starting on the A note and ending on the next higher A note.

Below is a table that shows the Major keys with their corresponding sharps and flats along with the relative minor for each major key.

Ex. 13

Flat Keys

Key	Flats	Notes That Are Flatted	Relative Minor
F	1	B	Dm
B♭	2	B & E	Gm
E♭	3	B, E & A	Cm
A♭	4	B, E, A & D	Fm
D♭	5	B, E, A, D & G	B♭m
G♭	6	B, E, A, D, G & C	E♭m
C♭	7	B, E, A, D, G, C & F	A♭m

Sharp Keys

Key	Sharps	Notes That Are Sharped	Relative Minor
G	1	F	Em
D	2	F & C	Bm
A	3	F, C & G	F#m
E	4	F, C, G & D	C#m
B	5	F, C, G, D & A	G#m
F#	6	F, C, G, D, A & E	D#m
C#	7	F, C, G, D, A, E & B	A#m

Note that some keys are enharmonic (the same pitches with different spelling). Ex. F# = G♭.

Travelin' Man Blues - CD Track 1 (Examples: Track 18)

Key: E

Groove: Shuffle (Jimmy Reed style)

Tempo: 108bpm (beats per minute)

Intro: From the V (4 measure intro before the standard twelve bar form starts). Chord Symbols (B) and Roman Numerals (V) are included to show which chord these lines are played to.

Body: 6 Choruses of standard **12 Bar Blues** (Body refers to the main form/chord progression of the song).

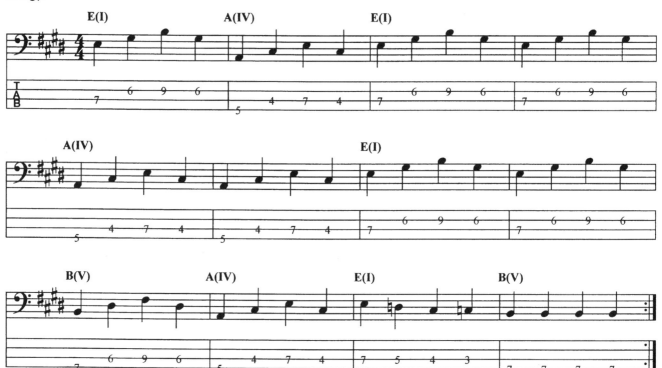

Ending: Band breaks on the downbeat of the 11th measure (I chord) in the sixth chorus. This and the following ending examples will start from the 9th measure to give you a little bit more context than just the last two measures. There is a slight ritard at the end (slowing down).

Comments:
A great simple shuffle with a pattern that bass players can use for multiple shuffle type songs.

Muddy's Shuffle - CD Track 2 (Examples: Track 19)

Key: G

Groove: Shuffle (Bass line is what a common Muddy Waters song would use, thus the name)

Tempo: 108bpm

Intro: From the Turnaround (2 measure intro before the standard twelve bar form starts). The keyboard leads in, with the band coming in for two notes before the form begins.

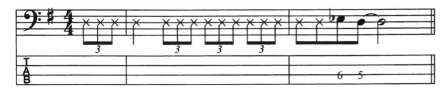

Body: 6 Choruses of standard **12 Bar Blues**. Notice the nice hook played by the guitar and organ.

Break: A break is used on the first four measures of the third and sixth choruses.

Ending: Break on the 10th measure (IV chord), coming back in on the 11th measure (I chord).

In The Box - CD Track 3 (Examples: Track 20)

Key: G

Groove: Shuffle (What is commonly referred to as an ascending box)

Tempo: 120bpm

Body: 8 Choruses of standard **12 Bar Blues**

Ending: Band uses standard break on the downbeat of the 11th measure (I chord). Soloist will play the break section (silent area between the 11th and 12th measures).

Comments:

This is a great shuffle pattern that is not used very often. This pattern has a smooth sound and it is a rocker! Try using this pattern in a standard shuffle, but be sure the guitar player is not going to play a bass line (this will conflict with your line). This pattern sounds really good with a little more low end added and a little high end rolled off.

Mr. Green - CD Track 4 (Examples: Track 21)

Key: F minor (Lower case roman numerals are used to indicate minor chords)

Groove: Green Onions/Help Me

Tempo: 138bpm

Intro: Organ plays for 4 bars, then the band starts on the i chord (beginning of the 12 Bar Blues form).

Body: 6 Choruses of **12 Bar Blues**.

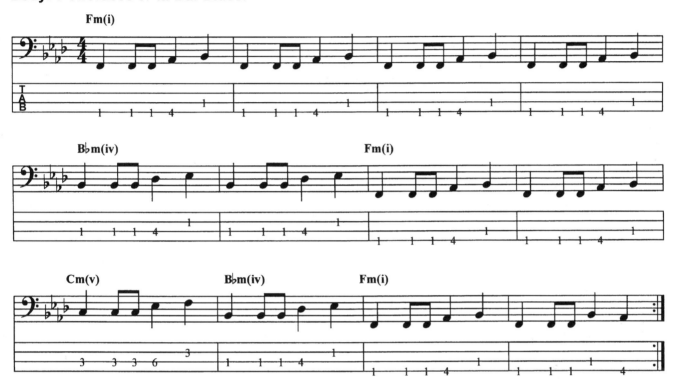

Ending: At the end of the sixth chorus repeat the last four bars.

Comments:

This is a groove that is best played simply and steadily with a deep, rich tone. A simple and steady bass line allows plenty of room for the rhythms and accents played by the drums, organ and guitar to stand out.

Minor Problem - CD Track 5 (Examples: Track 22)

Key: C minor

Groove: Slow Blues with triplet feel

Tempo: 60bpm

Intro: One beat pickup from the band into the beginning of the form.

Body: 4 Choruses of **12 Bar Blues**. Though a 12 bar form, it is not standard. There is no iv chord at the 5th measure, giving eight measures of the i chord. Instead of a minor v and iv, a major V and IV are used for a nice change of color. There is also no turnaround (the i chord is played for the 11th and 12th measures).

Ending: Band uses standard break on the downbeat of the 11th measure. An ending lick like what's notated below will work nice (note the major I chord). There is a ritard at the end.

Comments:
A slow blues with a very interesting form and nice strong hook played by the guitar and piano.

Major Problem - CD Track 6 (Examples: Track 23)

Key: G

Groove: Slow Blues with triplet feel

Tempo: 64bpm

Body: 4 Choruses of standard **12 Bar Blues**

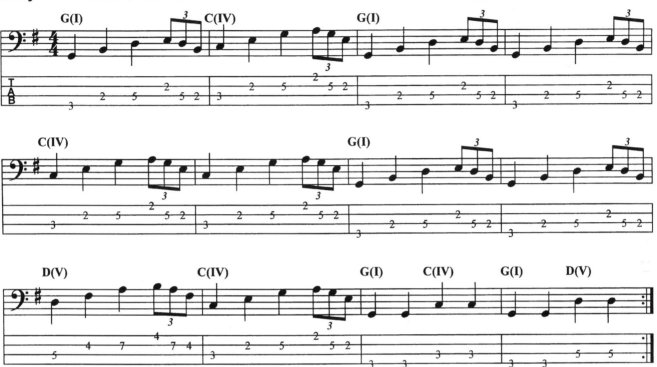

Ending: Band uses standard break on the downbeat of the 11th measure with a stylized line that has a slight ritard at the end.

Comments:

This slow blues has all the fundamental elements of a traditional urban blues song. The triplets on the guitar help to enhance this slow blues, though this bass pattern can be played to a slow blues that does not feature the triplets. When playing a slow blues that features triplets as a consistent rhythmic pattern, the bass player and drummer lock in and hold the tempo in place by playing mostly quarter notes.

Charlie's Swing - CD Track 7 (Examples: Track 24)

Key: B♭

Groove: Uptown Swing with Charleston feel

Tempo: 210bpm

Body: 11 Choruses of **12 Bar Blues** with jazzy changes.

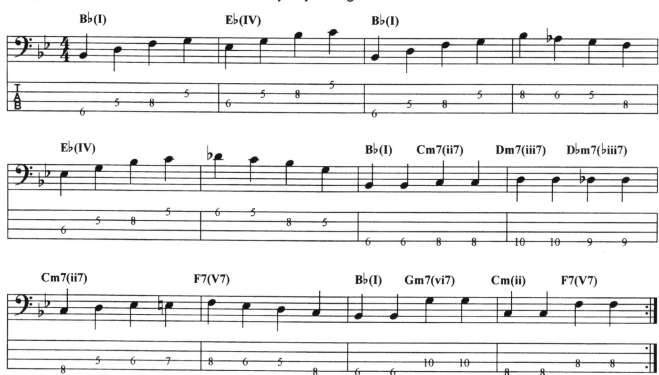

Ending: The last four measures repeat for a total of three times with a break at the end.

Uptown Jump - CD Track 8 (Examples: Track 25)

Key: F

Groove: Upbeat Jump with backwards shuffle on the drums

Tempo: 122bpm

Intro: From the ii (4 measure intro before the standard twelve bar form starts).

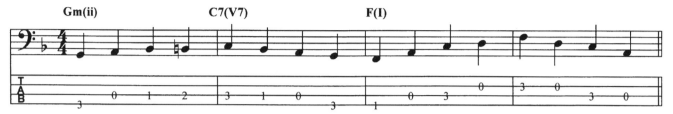

Body: 10 Choruses of standard **12 Bar Blues**.

Break: A break is used on the first four measures of the fifth chorus. You can use the line below.

Ending: Band uses standard break on the downbeat of the 11th measure with a unison lick.

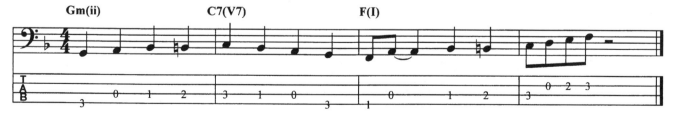

The Stroll - CD Track 9 (Examples: Track 26)

Key: F

Groove: Stroll

Tempo: 108bpm

Intro: Piano starts with band playing swing eighths at the end.

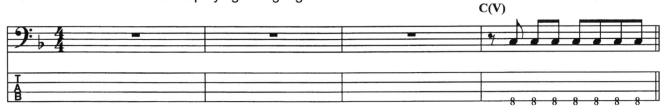

Body: 6 Choruses of an **8 Bar Blues**

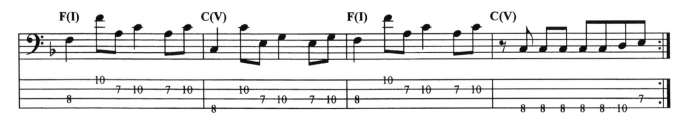

Ending: Band breaks on the downbeat of the 7th measure (common for an 8 bar blues).

Comments:

I love to play a stroll, especially with a great piano player like Steve Czarnecki. This track really swings. Everyone is playing their simple parts to perfection. Pay close attention to John Garcia's guitar part; it is the perfect counterpoint to the piano.

If you are the bass player in a blues band with a piano player, you will need to spend some time together working out your parts. A good blues piano player plays with two hands. This means that the two of you will play the bass patterns together on many songs. When you are not playing in unison, your line needs to be simple and consistent so the piano player can develop a counterpoint line that enhances the song by filling out the chords and the rhythm.

The Key - CD Track 10 (Examples: Track 27)

Key: G

Groove: Shuffle

Tempo: 96bpm

'Key To The Highway'

Intro: From the Turnaround.

Body: 6 Choruses of an **8 Bar Blues**

Option for Last 4 Measures: Try this line as well in place of the last four measures of the previous example.

Ending: Band breaks on the downbeat of the 7th measure.

Comments:

8 Bar Blues come in many different forms, though this and "The Stroll" presents the most common versions. It's a good idea to work on these until you are comfortable playing them. Though 12 Bar Blues is the most common, 8 Bar Blues is not uncommon.

Good Mojo - CD Track 11 (Examples: Track 28)

Key: E

Groove: 2 Beat

Tempo: 126bpm is the tempo, though the 2 Beat groove makes it feel twice as fast. For this reason it is sometimes called a cut shuffle.

Intro: From the Turnaround.

Body: 8 Choruses of standard **12 Bar Blues**.

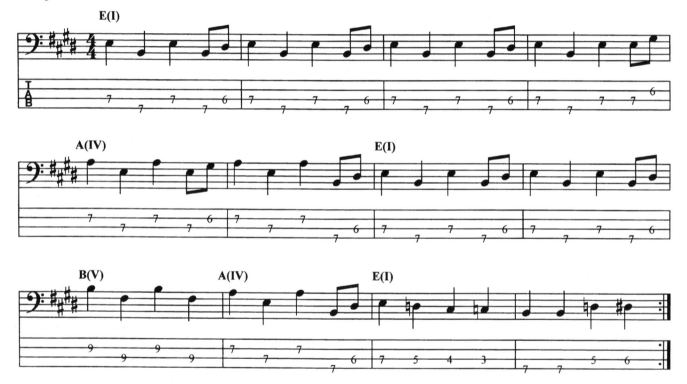

Ending: Band breaks on the downbeat of the 10th measure (IV chord) with the band coming back in on the 11th measure (I chord). You can use a lick like what is notated below.

Comments:
This pattern is a must-have in your bag of tricks. This groove is best when played simply and solidly.

Mr. Rhumba - CD Track 12 (Examples: Track 29)

Key: A

Groove: Rhumba (Rhumba uses straight eights. It is not a shuffle or swing rhythm)

Tempo: 126bpm

Intro: From the V.

Body: 8 Choruses of standard **12 Bar Blues**.

On the fourth and fifth chorus the groove moves to a **Shuffle**. You could play the line below.

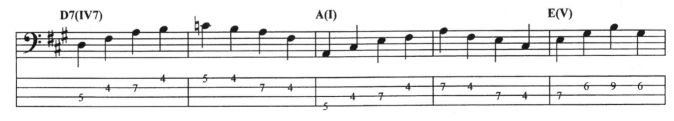

19

Ending: The band plays the V three times at the end (the last four measures three times) with a "Cha Cha Cha" at the very end.

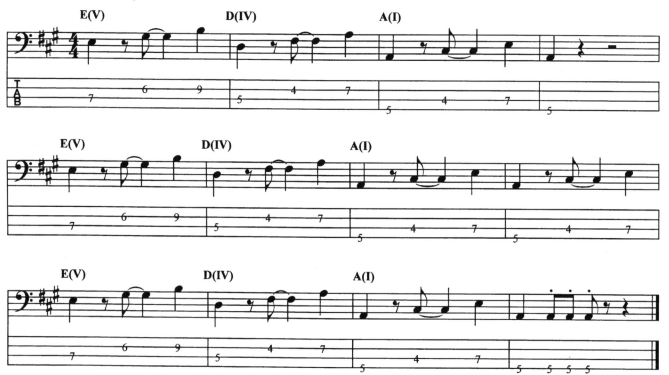

Comments:

The rhumba is a mainstay in every modern blues band. This is a nice and simple rhumba with a shuffle section added. The beauty of a rhumba is that the complex syncopated sound is created by the composite effect of each instrument playing very simple parts. This bass pattern is the foundation of a good rhumba. Play it simply and repetitively and you will create the groove that is at the heart of this syncopated sound.

Boogie - CD Track 13 (Examples: Track 30)

Key: A

Groove: Boogie

Tempo: 144bpm

Intro: Guitar plays a 4 bar intro. You will enter after the intro.

Form: This is a modal blues. Modal means that the entire song is based on the I chord of a given scale (mode). In other words, there is no chord change like the others grooves we have played so far.

Groove Pattern: A 1 bar pattern

Walking Pattern: A 4 bar pattern

Ending Pattern: A 4 bar pattern. Play the root note (E) for the last two hits of the band.

Structure:
4 Bars Guitar Only
20 Bars Groove Pattern
8 Bars Bass Walking Pattern (4 Bar Pattern Twice)
8 Bars Groove Pattern
8 Bars Bass Walking Pattern
52 Bars Groove Pattern
8 Bars Ending Pattern
Finish with two hits of the root note (E)

Comments:
Everyone loves the one chord boogie! This is a powerful groove, like a locomotive train. Harp players and guitar players love the boogie. From John Lee Hooker, to Canned Heat, to ZZ Top, everyone pays tribute to the boogie. Dial in a big, deep bass sound and play your simple line with emotion and precision. You and the drummer need to hold this hypnotic groove in place, otherwise the song will speed up.

The Tramp - CD Track 14 (Examples: Track 31)

Key: C

Groove: Funk Beat (Non-shuffle rhythm, straight eight notes)

Tempo: 116bpm

Body: 6 Choruses of standard **12 Bar Blues**

Ending: Band breaks on the downbeat of the 12th measure.

Comments:

The tramp groove is a great dance beat. The audience always loves this groove. Keep your bass patterns steady and in the pocket and the dance floor will be crowded. Also, by playing a simple pattern like the one above, you leave plenty of room for the drummer to get funky. And, when the drummer gets funky, your simple bass line sounds great.

Little Bit - CD Track 15 (Examples: Track 32)

Key: D

like Birthday by the Beatles

Groove: Rock Beat (Non-shuffle rhythm, straight eight notes)

Tempo: 168bpm

Body: 4 Choruses of standard **12 Bar Blues**

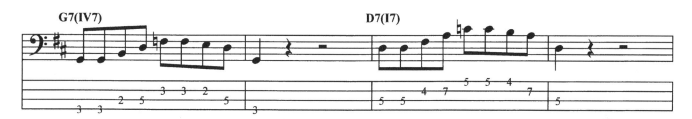

Option 2: Notated below is what is played for the second and third choruses.

Thanks To...

I want to thank my wife Peggy and my daughter Bianca for the many years of support and understanding of my endless pursuit of playing the blues. I want to thank blues harmonica great Gary Smith for teaching me the blues. I want to thank the teachers at the School of the Blues for their great performances on the musical tracks on this CD. And I want to thank them for their inspiration and sharing of their musical knowledge with me. They are Kevin Coggins on drums, John Garcia on guitar and Steve Czarnecki on piano and organ. And lastly I want to thank David Barrett. Not only is he a great harmonic player but he is also the owner of the School of the Blues. This book would not have been possible without David and the School of the Blues.

- Producer, Editor & Co-Author – David Barrett
- Musicians – The following musicians performed on the recording.
  - John Garcia (All guitar and vocal work)
  - Frank De Rose (Bass)
  - Kevin Coggins (Drums)
  - Steve Czarnecki (Organ & Piano)
  - Recorded at Soundtek Studios in Campbell, California. Engineered by Thom Duell.
  - Narration and bass recordings done at School of the Blues® in San Jose, California.
- Context Proof Readers
  - Dennis Carelli, Scott Clay & Jack Sanford
- Photography – Dave Lepori Photography in San Jose, California

School of the Blues Staff
Front Row (L-R): Frank De Rose, John Garcia and Kevin Coggins
Back Row (L-R): Steve Czarnecki and David Barrett

Made in the USA
Monee, IL
10 August 2020